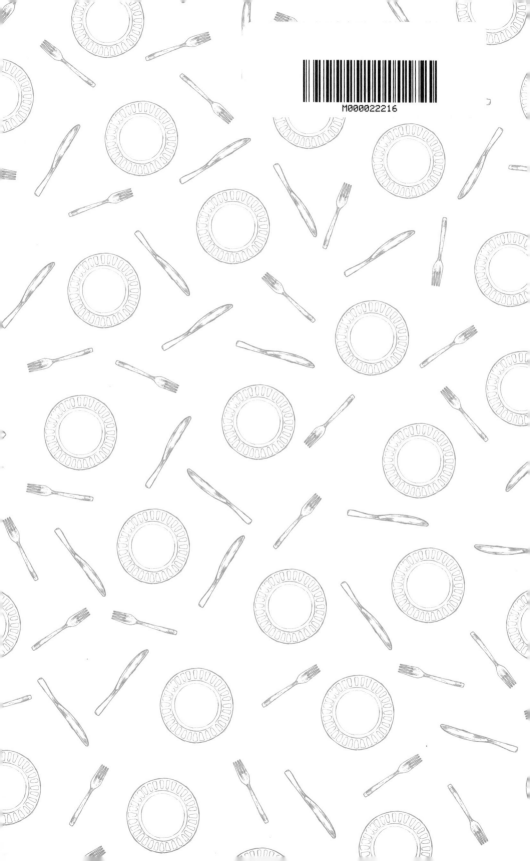

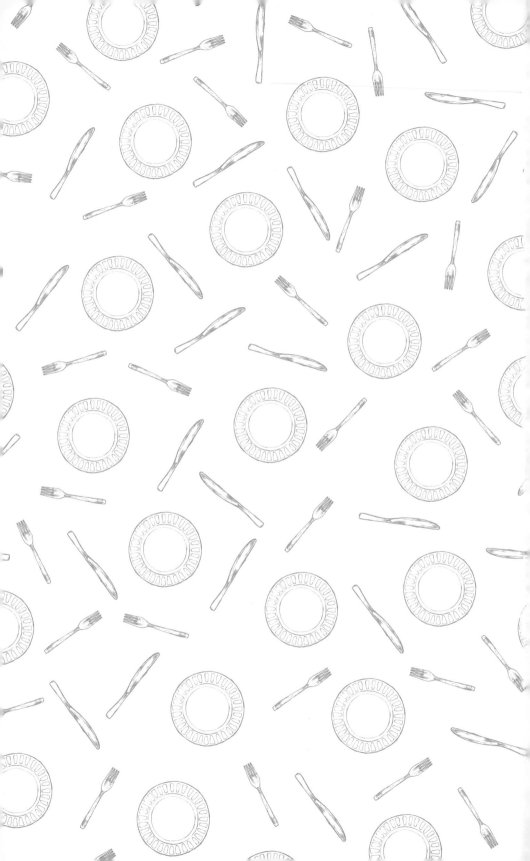

BECAUSE HE FIRST FED US

Never underestimate the
power of a good meal !
Anita McVey

Hebrews 13:2

BECAUSE HE FIRST FED US

ANITA HINKELDEY MCVEY

ROMANS 8:28
BOOKS

...all things work together for good...

AN IMPRINT OF REDEMPTION PRESS

© 2021 by Anita Hinkeldey McVey. All rights reserved.

Published by Romans 8:28 Books, PO Box 427, Enumclaw, WA 98022.
Toll-Free (844) 2REDEEM (273-3336)

Romans 8:28 Books is honored to present this title in partnership with the author. The views expressed or implied in this work are those of the author. Redemption Press provides our imprint seal representing design excellence, creative content, and high-quality production.

The author has tried to recreate events, locales, and conversations from memories of them. In order to maintain their anonymity, in some instances the names of individuals, some identifying characteristics, and some details may have been changed, such as physical properties, occupations, and places of residence.

Noncommercial interests may reproduce portions of this book without the express written permission of the author, provided the text does not exceed five hundred words. When reproducing text from this book, include the following credit line: "*Because He First Fed Us* by Anita Hinkeldey McVey. Used by permission."

Commercial interests: No part of this publication may be reproduced in any form, stored in a retrieval system, or transmitted in any form by any means—electronic, photocopy, recording, or otherwise—without prior written permission of the publisher/author, except as provided by United States of America copyright law.

All Scripture quotations are from the Holy Bible, New International Version®, NIV®. Copyright © 1973, 1978, 1984, 2011 by Biblica, Inc.™ Used by permission of Zondervan. All rights reserved worldwide. www.zondervan.com The "NIV" and "New International Version" are trademarks registered in the United States Patent and Trademark Office by Biblica, Inc.™

ISBN 13: 978-1-64645-025-1

Library of Congress Catalog Card Number: 2021917234

As a self-proclaimed foodie, few flavors create a bad taste in my mouth. One, however, absolutely disgusts me—the taste of my own foot after I have inadvertently shoved it into my mouth with misplaced words. I've tasted that unfortunate flavor many times because my enthusiasm for talking gets way ahead of my brain and my heart. If I have said anything in this book that was shortsighted, single-minded, or even the slightest bit insulting, I pray that you know it was not intentional, and I ask your forgiveness.

Come on In!

||||||||||||||||||||||||||||||||||||||||||||||

Cooking is love made visible is one of my favorite sayings. As a child, I witnessed this love at the side of my mom and my grandmothers. As a wife and mother, I carried out this love for my family. Many, many times this love was how I showed my sympathies and my concern for others. But in the past ten to fifteen years, I have become completely enamored with cooking. Even more than that, I am positively enchanted by food.

To me, food is a love language. It nourishes, heals, comforts, and delights the body and the soul. The way to make delicious food even better: share it. When food is transformed into a meal, it becomes love in action. All the senses are engaged: sight, sound, taste, touch, and smell. Memories are revived. Stories are told. Gratitude is expressed. Conversations flow and wisdom is gleaned. Even the dirty dishes have a story to tell (see page 64).

Before God created mankind, He created a garden. God was preparing a meal for us before we arrived. He gave us our senses to fully appreciate and enjoy this world. He gave us our family and friends and the opportunities to share with each other and with strangers. And He gave us His Word.

God speaks to us in the love language of food. He knows we will comprehend and remember His teachings when they are relatable. And this is how this book came to be.

God started revealing small details in Scripture to me in subtle ways. Listening to readings at church, hearing the word *cucumber* spoken, and thinking, "I've never heard cucumbers mentioned in the Bible before!" (Numbers 11:5). Looking through old church cookbooks, I'd find a recipe from one of the ladies I knew, and a memory of her would prompt a story. This book created itself over the past five years. Well . . . let's be honest . . . God created this book, and it took me five years to write it.

Many people question why God doesn't speak to us as He spoke to people in the Bible. If you tell people that God does speak to you, they may do a quick about-face or subtle eye roll. I can honestly say that God spoke to me directly and clearly many times in this process. Whether it was the nudge of hearing the word *cucumber* from a pulpit or waking up with the exact word I had struggled to find the day before, I heard Him. There were mornings where I woke early to the words "get up." After burying myself in the covers, the words returned. Sometimes I pushed my luck until the third round of instruction came, before forcing myself out of the bed. As the coffee brewed, I'd grab my laptop and the words would pour out.

This book is my way of sharing a meal with you. As you read, my prayer is that you will laugh at my expense, learn from my mistakes, discover new and wonderful messages from the Bible, and your soul will be fed.

Come, Lord Jesus, be our guest
And let these gifts to us be blessed.
Amen.

Contents

1. A Place of Honor 10
2. Adventures in Eating 12
3. An Impromptu Dinner Party 14
4. The Bad-News Sandwich 16
5. Breakfast on the Beach 18
6. Cream or Sugar? 20
7. Dead to the World 22
8. For the Love of Pizza 24
9. Fruit Salad 26
10. God's Cookbook 28
11. Kid in a Candy Store 30
12. Kitchen Scraps 32
13. A Hangry Field Trip 34
14. Glass Half-Full 36
15. Picnic Baskets 38
16. Lemonade Stands 40
17. The Lifesaving Delivery 42
18. Lunchroom Drama 44
19. Muscle Memory 46
20. Omitting Ingredients 48
21. Pancake Sundays 50
22. Quarts, Pints, and Jelly Jars 52
23. Regretfully Decline or Joyfully Accept? 54
24. Set an Extra Place at the Table 56
25. Stars and Candy Bars 58
26. Stone Soup 60
27. Superpowers 62
28. The Dishwashing Feud 64
29. The Essential Pantry 66
30. Wise Menu Choices 68
Gratitude 70

A Place of Honor

|||||||||||||||||||||||||||||||||||||

Luke 14:7–11

I think most families who make a practice of eating meals together at a table fall into a routine of a single seating arrangement. Intentional or not, each person has *their* spot. When guests arrive, they often ask, "Where would you like me to sit?" At large family gatherings, it's a big deal to move from the kids' table to the adults' table.

As I was growing up, our home had a peninsula-style table. Similar to a peninsula countertop, this table extended from the wall and abutted the end of our kitchen cabinets. Mom sat in the spot right next to the cabinets so she could easily grab silverware, plates, or more food. My dad sat across from her. To my dad's left sat my oldest brother. To my mom's right sat my brother, the second oldest. That left two spots at the table. One on the end and between my brothers (who are eight and nine years older than me) and one to my dad's right. I wanted to be as far away from my brothers as possible. It is fair to say my brothers would have preferred I would sit next to my dad too. It would give them more leg room!

But that was not a decision for us to make. My dad liked to have his newspapers, farm magazines, bills, and mail next to him so he could do a little business after a meal and before going back outside to work. So the three of us sat together at the end of the table.

Jesus used the topic of seating arrangements to teach some Pharisees a lesson. He described a scene from one of their feasts by pointing out how the guests tried to position themselves in places where they would be noticed. The arrogance of this posturing set the guests up for humiliation should they be asked to move. In other words, they would receive a very public and embarrassing attitude adjustment.

> *For all those who exalt themselves will be humbled, and those who humble themselves will be exalted.* (Luke 14:11)

It is human nature to try to rank our sins on a scale, comparing our infractions to others'. By doing so, we "choose a place of honor" that we do not deserve. Sin is more than a mistake or infraction. We cannot establish a system of ranking or tallying our wrongs or the wrongs of others. Sin is a condition. We all have it. We are all equally guilty and equally forgiven. Humility is our only option.

Whether or not my parents ever intended to establish a humble mealtime seating arrangement, my brothers and I knew our place . . . equally and completely loved.

Dear God,
Thank You for the invitation to
Your heavenly banquet. I know I do
not deserve to attend, but I humbly
accept. I leave all my arrogance
and self-centeredness at the door
and enter into the celebration of
eternal life.
Amen.

Adventures in Eating

|||||||||||||||||||||||||||||||||||||||||||||||

Matthew 3:1–6

In the past fifteen years, I have become an adventurous eater. When we eat at a restaurant, I am likely to choose something new on the menu. If we are traveling, I will search out restaurants that serve food unique to the region. Browsing ethnic grocery stores or strolling through farmers' markets piques my curiosity. My family knows they can give me gifts of obscure spices, cookbooks, and cooking utensils, and I will love them!

This is one case where television has had a positive effect on my life. Some wonderful cooking shows have whet this adventurous spirit. Some shows feature chefs from around the world. When chefs are forced to cook with unfamiliar ingredients (both to them and to me), the attributes of that ingredient come to life. Those episodes entice me to open my mind (and stomach) to new food sources.

Would you believe I am even open to eating bugs? It's totally okay if you think I have lost my mind, but please keep reading. Around the world, entomophagy, or the practice of eating insects, is common. Beetles, worms, and insects are a complete protein loaded with vitamins, minerals, amino acids, and fiber. One chef in particular, who travels the world eating anything and everything they put in front of him, compared the taste of one insect to shrimp and another to almonds.

Still not interested?

Just as my curiosity was intrigued by the unusual cooking skills and eating habits of these television chefs, the people of Judea and Galilee were curious about a man named John the Baptist.

> *John's clothes were made of camel's hair, and he had a leather belt around his waist. His food was locusts and wild honey. People went out to him from Jerusalem and the whole region of the Jordan. (Matthew 3:4–5)*

Born months before Jesus, John's arrival and name was announced by angels. They told John's parents that he would prepare the way for Jesus, the Messiah. John lived his life in the desert, and his diet was bugs and honey.

We could speculate on the nutritional elements of his diet or debate whether he ate other foods. There are many theories on this seven-word passage in Scripture. The important point is that John lived an uncomplicated life. He was devoted completely to the preaching and teaching of salvation through Jesus Christ.

Consider how much time you spend thinking about what you will have to eat for your next meal. Then add the time spent buying groceries, preparing the meal, and washing the dishes. If those decisions and that effort were removed from your day, how much time could you spend focusing on your relationship with God? Examining how we spend our time might reveal places to simplify and reprioritize. We may also discover ways to glorify God in our everyday tasks. You can follow John the Baptist's example even if you choose not to become an entomophagist.

I still think the chocolate-covered crickets can't be all bad.

Dear God,
You created a beautiful and complex world full of opportunity. You give me my passions and my work. Help me always to follow John's example of living for You and sharing the story of salvation wherever I go. Amen.

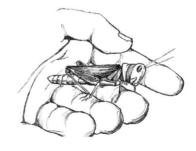

An Impromptu Dinner Party

||||||||||||||||||||||||||||||||||||||||||||||||||||

Luke 10:38–42

Dinner parties, family reunions, holiday gatherings . . . does the idea of serving ten, twelve, or twenty people a meal in your home instantly cause your mind to race? Do questions of what to serve, how many tables you need, and when you last cleaned the bathrooms pop into your head? Making people feel welcome and comfortable is an ambitious task even if you are a hostess at heart.

When Jesus's friend Martha hears that Jesus and His disciples are passing through her town, she invites them to her home. She knows they will need a place to eat, rest, share their experiences, and continue to learn from their Teacher. We often associate the word *disciples* with the twelve men Jesus first called to follow him—the apostles. At this point in His ministry, many more people had become devoted followers of Jesus—disciples. In the tenth chapter of Luke (v. 1 and v. 17), Jesus appointed and sent seventy-two others ahead of him to the cities and towns to spread the gospel and perform miracles. Martha just committed herself to the care and nourishment of seventy-some guests.

If Jesus came to my house and brought seventy-two of His best buddies, I am quite certain I would be overcome with panic and anxiety. Full-on hostess-with-the-mostest mode would ensue, and it would not be pretty.

I find it almost comical how in verse 38, Martha "opened her home to him" and only two verses later she is complaining to Jesus

14

about being overwhelmed. Martha's sister, Mary, wasn't helping with the preparations. Instead, Mary took a rare opportunity to physically be with her friend, her Lord, and sat down to *listen* to Him. Oh, how I long to believe I would be a Mary in this situation, but I'm quite certain I would be a Martha.

Isn't it a relief that we don't have to worry about this scenario? Or do we?

> *For where two or three gather in my name, there am I with them. (Matthew 18:20)*

Jesus is sitting at our tables when there are two, three, ten, twenty or, yes, even seventy-five. Where is our focus? Is it on the preparations? Is it on the television or our phones? Do we jump up from the table to gather and wash the dishes, putting an abrupt end to any conversation in progress?

Jesus has proven to us repeatedly that He will provide. There *will* be enough food. We *will* have help doing the dishes (even if we have to ask for it). Our attentiveness, compassion, and laughter will stay with our guests long after their stomachs growl again. When our focus is on Him and the people He has put at our physical and metaphorical table, we will not lack a thing.

Gather, pray, share, eat, drink, and be present. Jesus will reveal Himself to us in those moments.

Dear Jesus,
You are the perfect Host. You are always
present, always providing, and always
attentive. Forgive me when I get distracted
by what I think I should do, and draw me
into that intimate conversation with You.
Amen.

THE BAD-NEWS SANDWICH

||||||||||||||||||||||||||||||||||||||||||||||

John 13:1–14:2

After publishing a blog about a mini-vacation my husband and I had taken, two people reached out to let me know I had misspelled the name of one of the small towns we'd visited. The first message simply stated my error. No pleasantries exchanged. No accusations of stupidity or negligence either. Just a statement. There was nothing wrong with that message, but my guard went up, and I immediately felt defensive. The second message arrived shortly after the first, and it also pointed out my error, but it started with a single word about the article itself that made me smile: "Loved." It also ended by assuming the typo was unintentional.

This second message used what is known as the Bad-News Sandwich approach. Conceptually, difficult news (the meat) is easier to receive when it is surrounded by positive reinforcement (the bread). If the recipient feels loved, appreciated, and respected, the meat is easier to swallow (pun intended).

It may seem outrageous to compare the Passover Feast to a sandwich, but when Jesus and His disciples gather to honor this tradition in Jerusalem, He has some bad news to share with them. Jesus demonstrates a powerful lesson in how to approach, deliver, and conclude an uncomfortable, yet unavoidable, conversation.

Rather than launching into the conversation with a tirade, ticking off each issue on his fingers, Jesus begins with compassion. In fact, He leads with a gesture. He humbles Himself before them and washes their feet. Aren't we more apt to listen to someone who approaches us with love and humility rather than accusation and condescension?

The bad news Jesus shares with the disciples creates more of a giant hoagie than a simple sandwich. Calmly, He delivers the messages the apostles weren't expecting.

Layer one: He identifies Judas as the one who will betray Him. Layer two: He predicts Peter's denial. Layer three: Before any of them start pointing fingers, He reveals that they will all abandon Him. Layer four: Jesus would soon be leaving them.

Imagine the sadness, frustration, and fear around that table. There was also a healthy spread of denial, indignation, and guilt. In His great mercy and kindness, Jesus does not leave them to wallow in that emotional state. The sandwich is completed with an affirmation: the promise of forgiveness and the resurrection.

> *Do not let your hearts be troubled. You believe in God; believe also in me. My Father's house has many rooms; if that were not so, would I have told you that I am going there to prepare a place for you? (John 14:1–2)*

If we choose to employ Jesus's example in our day-to-day interactions with others, just imagine the results. Lead with humility, kindness, and a calm voice (or gesture). Be honest and empathetic. Love others as brothers and sisters in Christ. An invitation to grab a sandwich is often a good place to start.

Dear Jesus,
You show me unending compassion,
unlimited patience, and undeserved
grace. Help me to approach each
day and each person following Your
example. May they see You in how
I choose my words and actions.
Amen.

5

Breakfast on the Beach

|||||||||||||||||||||||||||||||||||||||||||||

John 21:1–14

If I say "breakfast on the beach," do you immediately imagine yourself reclining in a beach chair? Are you stretched out in the warm morning sun? Is there a tray of fruits, muffins, and coffee ... or maybe a beverage with a pretty, little umbrella ... next to you that was delivered by a member of the resort staff? Welcome to paradise!

Or maybe you imagine yourself getting out of a boat after returning from an early morning fishing expedition. Part of the resort's package includes breakfast on the shoreline. You sit back, drink a hot cup of coffee, and watch as that morning's catch is prepared for you. Any devoted angler will tell you, nothing tastes better than a meal of freshly caught fish prepared on shore by your guide.

We can all imagine different scenarios, but I think we can agree the phrase *breakfast on the beach* sounds mighty inviting. Throughout the Gospels, Jesus and His disciples are often found on or around a body of water. In the passage from John, we read about a special morning where Jesus found the disciples by the Sea of Tiberias.

It is important to understand that at this time Jesus had been crucified and had reportedly risen from the dead. Adding to the disciples' confusion, Jesus had appeared to some but not all of them (v. 14). I cannot begin to comprehend how confusing these events must have been. Perhaps, feeling the need to clear their heads, they decided to do what they did best. They went fishing. Before Jesus called them to follow Him, fishing had been their livelihood. It was hard and dirty work. As you may know, it is no fun at all if you don't catch any fish (v. 3).

Imagine the eye rolls when a stranger on the beach yelled out advice, instructing them to try the other side of the boat. I think that is the equivalent of a parent yelling "Just throw strikes!" to their child who is struggling on the mound during a baseball game (not that I would know anything about that). Imagine the shock when the nets filled and the light-bulb moment when they realized that their friend, Jesus, was guiding them from the shore! The ever-exuberant Peter jumps in the water and swims to shore, unable to contain his joy. The others towed the overflowing nets to shore.

> *When they landed, they saw a fire of burning coals there with fish on it, and some bread. (John 21:9)*

In a short time, Jesus would ascend into heaven and the disciples would carry out their commission to tell the world about the Savior. He physically served them one more time that morning. He made breakfast for them (v. 9) right there on the beach.

Jesus is our guide. Sometimes we recognize Him and sometimes we don't. We are His disciples sent to serve. He doesn't promise us a five-star experience here on earth. He does promise to prepare a place for us for all eternity in the most glorious of resorts.

Dear Jesus,
Thank You for turning the despair
I often feel into joy and being the
friend who comforts me and shows
me the way. May I always recognize
You and give You glory from the
"beach" on which I stand.
Amen.

CREAM OR SUGAR?

IIIIIIIIIIIIIIIIIIIIIIIIIIIIIIIIIIIIIII
Exodus 3:8

One of my favorite movies is an oldie (you know . . . from the '90s) called *You've Got Mail*. One popular scene takes place while Kathleen places her order in a coffee shop. She recalls a recent online chat conversation with the mysterious Joe. His mild rant on people who lack everyday decision-making skills ends with amazement over how easily those same people can order a complicated cup of coffee: ". . . short, tall . . . light, dark . . . caf, decaf . . . low-fat, nonfat . . . etc.!"

This scene runs through my head almost every time I am waiting in line for my "grande chai latte, no whip." Sometimes I add a shot of espresso just to make it even more complicated.

Remember when coffee was a simple drink? Ordering a cup at a restaurant or preparing one for a guest involved two questions: Would you like a cup? Cream or sugar? Oh, the comfort that came from sitting down, wrapping your hands around that warm mug, taking that first sip of perfectly sweetened and/or creamed goodness, and letting go of all the worries of the day.

Wouldn't it be wonderful if a simple cup of coffee could solve more than just our day-to-day worries? We picture the strife and crises that plague our modern world and feel so lost.

When these feelings overwhelm us, the Word will comfort and rejuvenate us. In Exodus, God's people became slaves to the new king of Egypt, who feared their number and potential power. God promised to save the Israelites from their bitter captivity in the dry desert.

> *So I have come down to rescue them from the hand of the Egyptians and to bring them up out of that land into a good and spacious land, a land flowing with milk and honey—*
> *(Exodus 3:8)*

Does that mean the rivers and streams of this promised land were a source of coffee enhancements? Of course not. Healthy animals are the source of milk. Bees collect nectar to make honey. Therefore, lush pastures and flower pollen must be present. This verse is a promise of opportunity, provision, and abundance for the Israelites. It is a vision of fertile land and the ability to grow what is needed.

Milk and honey are used symbolically throughout the Bible to emphasize the attributes of a living faith. How sweet it is to understand and savor God's Word (Psalm 119:103). Listen to God and follow His directions, and all our needs will be provided (Psalm 81:16). Choosing to speak pleasant words is a healing practice (Proverbs 16:24). Pray for wisdom (Proverbs 24:13–14) and discernment (Isaiah 7:15) to make the right decisions. When we work to filter our minds, straining out destructive and negative thoughts and filling up with what is good and right and constructive, the Spirit grows in us (1 Peter 2:1–2).

Embracing these attributes, we understand prosperity as God defines it. Bitterness cannot live in us. Our lives are sweeter. Each day has the appeal of a tall, full-fat cup of joy . . . with a shot of espresso, of course.

Dear God,
Remove from me all bitterness.
Please fill my cup with what I need
to do Your will today. May I always
pause to give thanks for the milk and
honey You add to my life.
Amen.

DEAD TO THE WORLD
||||||||||||||||||||||||||||||||||||||||||||
Mark 5:21–43

Have you ever tried to wake a child, especially a teenager, at an ungodly hour? You know . . . like before 9:00 a.m.? A grunt or groan might pass as, "I heard you, now leave me alone!" Any movement at all is considered progress. Opening the curtains only forces the child deeper under the covers. It has been my experience that the smell of warm cinnamon rolls is the best way to coax "sleeping beauty" back to life.

The phrase "dead to the world" is often used to describe a soundly sleeping person who is difficult to wake. The smell of hot coffee is enough to entice me to leave the warmth of my bed. Tempt me with warm cinnamon rolls and I am likely to hop out with enthusiasm!

Jairus, a leader in the Jewish synagogue, had a twelve-year-old daughter who was very sick. He left his home, determined to find Jesus. Jairus had heard of Jesus's miraculous healings. Seeing Jairus's faith, Jesus agreed to make a house call. Delayed by crowds and another opportunity for a miraculous healing (vv. 25–34), Jesus and Jairus received news that the girl had died. Jesus looks to the devastated father and reminds him that faith goes beyond mortality, and they continue to the house.

Amid the crying and grief, Jesus makes the mourners laugh by saying the girl is merely sleeping. With only the parents and three of his disciples present, Jesus touches her and says,

> *Little girl, I say to you, get up! (Mark 5:41)*

If I were Jairus, I would be searching the child's face for the slightest movement: a twitch of an eyelid or a slight tremor of a muscle. Let there be no doubt, this girl got out of bed and walked around!

The final words of this passage captured my attention.

> *Give her something to eat. (Mark 5:43)*

Why would God inspire Mark to include this tidbit of information in Scripture? Jesus has just revealed God's glory by restoring life to a twelve-year-old girl, and He wants to make sure her parents don't forget to feed her?

Maybe, in performing this miracle, Jesus does not want the witnesses to forget that He is not only true God, but also true man. A man who understands loss, fear, grief, temptation, and life-sustaining needs like food.

Perhaps Jesus is drawing their attention to the fact that this girl is not going to fall ill again once He leaves. When a severe cold or the flu has left you weak, what is the first sign that you might be getting better? Feeling hungry. His departing words may have been the promise of a complete recovery.

Jesus knows great comfort comes in the form of a good meal. Great comfort also comes in the form of spiritual nourishment. Are you preparing meals of faith for your family? Do you take time each day to feed your soul? Do you create a balanced diet of prayer and God's Word?

Maybe it is time for us to wake up and smell the cinnamon rolls!

Dear Miraculous Lord,
It is often hard for me to find balance
between my spiritual and earthly
needs and responsibilities. Wake me
up to opportunities to glorify You
and to feed others. Thank You for the
comfort that comes from a good meal.
Amen.

For the Love of Pizza

||||||||||||||||||||||||||||||||||||||||||

Exodus 16

How often have you heard kids say, "I could eat pizza every single day!" Honestly, I think I could too. There are so many choices when making or ordering pizza.

- What kind of crust? Thick or thin?
- What kind of sauce? Red or white?
- What kind of meat? Pepperoni, sausage, Canadian bacon, chicken, prosciutto?
- What kind of vegetables? Onions, peppers, mushrooms, olives, tomatoes, artichokes, arugula?
- What kind of cheese? Parmesan, mozzarella, cheddar, Asiago?

In a world of convenience and variety, it seems plausible we could eat nothing but pizza every day. But what if the variety is gone? What if the only kind of pizza was a thin-crust, red-sauce pizza with mozzarella? How long would eating the same pizza appeal to you?

A week? A month? A year?

Can I get a little pepperoni, *please*!

How about forty years?

When God rescued the Israelites from their slavery and oppression in Egypt, they had a problem with trusting that gave way to whining. They gave up on God and built themselves an idol. Rejecting God bought them forty years of wandering in the desert. They complained about their hunger and thirst until Moses pleaded with God on their behalf. God listened.

> *I have heard the grumbling of the Israelites. Tell them, "At twilight you will eat meat, and in the morning you will be filled with bread. Then you will know that I am the LORD your God." (Exodus 16:12)*

God *heard* them and *provided for* them morning and night. Manna, "thin flakes like frost" (v. 14) and "white like coriander seed and tasted like wafers made with honey" (v. 31), would appear on the ground in the morning for them to gather. Quail "covered the camp" each evening (v. 13). No hard labor required. Simply gather and prepare.

These free meals came with only one stipulation: gather only what was needed for the day. No leftovers, no excess, no midnight snacks. In fact, if someone decided they would prepare twice as much one day to ensure a meal for the next, the next morning it would be spoiled. God was teaching them to put complete trust in Him each day. Of course, they had to learn the hard way . . . waking up to smelly, maggot-filled leftovers (v. 20). Yet they also woke up to a fresh layer of manna. Even in their disobedience, God was faithful.

It is easy to shake our heads and roll our eyes at the Israelites' lack of faith and incessant complaining. But how long would it take for you to complain about thin-crust pizza with red sauce and mozzarella? A year? A month? A week?

I quickly join the ranks of the ungrateful and doubting. My complaining and desire to be in control have no place in my life as a Christian. Even in my most selfish and ungrateful moments, God hears my grumbling, and He provides for me. He hears you too, my friend, and He will provide for your needs.

Dear God,
Every single day You surround me with
all that is needed. Sometimes I am
grateful, but often I find myself whining
about what is missing in my life. Please
remind me every morning to gather only
what is needed for the day and remind me
every evening to thank You for your grace.
Amen.

FRUIT SALAD

|||||||||||||||||||||||||||||||||||||||||||||
Galatians 5:22–23

Making a fruit salad is not a complex task. The simplest of salads only require us to wash, cut, and combine the fruit in a bowl. We may choose a fancier bowl for serving company or even go to great effort carving a watermelon to look like a basket for special occasions, but the fruit inside is simple.

There really are no steadfast rules when it comes to making a fruit salad. In my opinion the best results come from an appealing mix of colors, flavors, and textures. Balance and proper preparation are the keys to success.

A bowl of grapes on the table can't really be considered a salad. Grapes are fruit and they are delicious, but alone they cannot be called a salad. Adding chunks of fresh pineapple to the bowl not only brings a new color but it also balances the sweetness of the grapes with some tartness. Strawberries and blueberries build on the rainbow of colors and provide interesting shapes to the mixture. A shot of citrus, like a squeeze of lemon or some mandarin oranges, brightens the salad.

Are you craving fruit now? Is this a salad you wish you had on your table right now? Would you like to be the type of person God would call a beautiful "fruit salad"?

> *But the fruit of the Spirit is love, joy, peace, forbearance, kindness, goodness, faithfulness, gentleness, and self-control. Against such things there is no law. (Galatians 5:22–23)*

Some days when I read this passage I am a mixture of love, kindness, and goodness. Other days I'm more gentle. Self-control comes and goes. Forbearance (i.e., patience) is seldom in my personal salad. I want to be a beautiful Christian. I try to incorporate all these attributes into my life and find that perfect balance of all nine characteristics. Honestly, there hasn't been even one single day when I have been able to achieve that goal.

Each one of us has one ingredient in our salad that throws off our balance: sin. Where there should be peace, we feel anger. The jealousy we have should be love. Self-control has been replaced with greed and faithfulness with self-centeredness. Life is not an easy recipe to perfect.

Praise God, the Holy Spirit is working in us and through us. When we prepare our hearts and minds with prayer and devotion, the Spirit is filling us. Studying Scripture until it rolls off our tongue brings us peace. Serving and forgiving others fills the space where greed and judgment try to live. Recognizing our imperfection and relying on our Savior eliminates arrogance and welcomes humility. Balance is restored.

God made you. Jesus has covered your imperfections. The Holy Spirit is shining inside you. You are a beautiful fruit salad.

Dear Loving Father,
Thank You for sending Jesus to remove
my sin and restore balance to my life.
Thank You for giving me Your Holy
Spirit to prepare my heart each day to be
more like You. May my life be a blessing
to others and a testament of love, joy,
peace, patience, kindness, generosity,
faithfulness, gentleness, and self-control.
Amen.

God's Cookbook

||||||||||||||||||||||||||||||||||||||||

John 20:31

I f you were required to eliminate all the cookbooks you own except one, which one would you keep? Would it be a hardbound book with stunning photos from your favorite chef or restaurant? Or maybe the spiral-bound collection of recipes that holds sentimental value to you because it was a gift from a special person? Is there one in particular that has inspired you to eat healthier?

Because I love cookbooks and have quite the collection, this decision would not make me happy. It would not be hard either. I would choose one without hesitation: the cookbook created to celebrate the centennial anniversary of the church of my childhood. It does not have pictures or a fancy cover. It has typos and stains and handwritten notes. Each recipe is followed by the name of the congregational member who submitted it. Each recipe tells a story about a family's traditions and tastes. This cookbook is forty years old, and I treasure it.

Church cookbooks are a wonderful way to learn to cook and bake. If there are any questions about one of the recipes, the solution is simple: ask the author. A quick phone call or post-worship conversation will produce the answer. Writing notes next to the recipe ensures the results will be even better the next time.

> *But these are written that you may believe that Jesus is the Messiah, the Son of God, and that by believing you may have life in His name. (John 20:31)*

I like to think about the Bible as God's cookbook: a collection of recipes for faith. Inspired by God, the authors of the Bible documented the miracles and signs, the trials and temptations, and the ever-present grace and love of the Father for us. Like following a recipe, the directions can sometimes feel incomplete or confusing. We may not always know how to apply Scripture to our daily life.

It is okay to ask for help. Do not hesitate to pray. Ask God to make it clear to you. Ask Him to show you the right steps. Ask a spiritual leader to explain what confuses you. Ask a faithful friend how they interpret and understand the directions. Let your Bible be stained with your fingerprints, filled with your notes, and soaked with your tears. The more familiar you become with the chapters and verses, the more your faith will grow and strengthen.

God's Word speaks to us. It feeds us and nourishes us. And like a favorite cookbook, the more time spent preparing the recipes, the more comfortable we are sharing them with others. We can give away the instructions. We can provide tips and explanations of what has worked well . . . and not so well . . . for us. We can celebrate with that person when they experience success too.

Perhaps over a piece of homemade pie.

Dear Author of the Living Word,
Thank You for having me in mind when
You inspired people like David and John
and Paul to write words of guidance and
inspiration and grace. May I always treat
each day as a recipe that comes from You,
and may I never be afraid to ask for help.
Amen.

KID IN A CANDY STORE

||||||||||||||||||||||||||||||||||||||||||

Genesis 2:1–24

What ever happened to candy stores? There are so few of those small shops with the glass cases displaying sweet, colorful candies. I imagine the owners do not enjoy cleaning those cases. After all, can't you just see those little faces breathing on the glass and the small hands pressed hard enough to capture every fingerprint?

Maybe it's worth it to the proprietors to see the eyes of wonder as kids try to decide what to choose. Will they point to the jar of jawbreakers? The bin of hard candies? Maybe a sticky sucker? It all looks so good!

Until the owner says "you can have whatever you want *except* the ones in *this* jar" and points to one big glass jar filled with an equally appealing option.

What is the child's natural reaction to this statement? Curiosity. The instantaneous *why?* In the blink of an eye, one forbidden candy becomes better looking, better tasting, and most desirable. Anyone else feel a tantrum building? Some parents might even be disgusted with the store owner for having something on display that isn't available. Wouldn't it be a happy ending if the child just trusted the owner and chose one of the other beautiful options? Temptation is tricky.

Adam and Eve were placed in the candy store of all candy stores—the garden of Eden. They had meaningful work without hard labor.

They walked with God and communed with nature. An endless buffet of food surrounded them. There was only one stipulation.

> *But you must not eat from the tree of the knowledge of good and evil, for when you eat from it you will certainly die. (Genesis 2:17)*

In Genesis 3, Satan draws Adam and Eve's attention back to that one tree. Using their curiosity to twist God's instruction, he slithers his way through a conversation that tempts them to disobey. In one bite of the forbidden "candy," they try to hide from God like a child hides to avoid the inevitable punishment.

Adam and Eve did receive punishment...banishment from Eden, hard labor, and eventually death. But with that punishment, God also made a promise. Their offspring would crush evil. Jesus would come to conquer death, to forgive sins, and to give eternal life to all who believe.

God is the owner of our candy-store life. He has filled the glass cases with wonderful things. He will protect us from the ultimate evil. He welcomes us and delights in every breath we take and in each fingerprint we leave. May our eyes always be filled with the wonder of our Creator and our trust be strengthened to follow His commands.

Dear God,
Your gifts surround me. You give me
more than I deserve, and You give me
choices. May my freewill always be
guided by Your Spirit. When I make
poor decisions, forgive me and teach
me how to forgive others in return.
Amen.

Kitchen Scraps

||||||||||||||||||||||||||||||||||||||||||||
Matthew 15:21–28

There are many rewards to working alongside a culinary expert. I like to say that I was "classically trained" by my mom, the 4-H organization, and the TV series *Chopped*. Three very different sources of education, but each instilled in me a respect and reverence for food. Implementing the tips and tricks they each offered has been a priceless pursuit. The best rewards often came in the form of the scraps.

Preserving fruit in the form of jelly or jam is an art. Prior to ladling the hot, syrupy, sweet substance into jars, a layer of foam must be skimmed from the top. This foam is created in the boiling process, and the air it contains can cause problems with the sealing and storage of the jars. It is often discarded. Spread on a piece of warm bread or toast, that foam is a coveted reward for helping with the canning process.

Learning to make piecrust from scratch is a challenge. Homemade pie for dessert will undoubtedly elicit sighs of appreciation. But what about those pieces of dough left over from trimming the crust? Roll them out, coat with a layer of butter, sprinkle with cinnamon and sugar, and bake the oddly shaped crust alongside the pie for a sweet compensation for hard work.

When it comes to barbecue, burnt ends are a delicacy. These charred cubes come from the fattier tip of a beef brisket that has been slow smoked, resulting in a tender and juicy bite. In high demand, burnt ends can be hard to find on menus. Would it surprise you to discover this coveted culinary portion of meat was once considered a scrap that was given away to customers while they waited for their food?

Recognizing the goodness that can be found in simple scraps was how one woman convinced Jesus to miraculously save her daughter. This woman was an outsider, a Canaanite. She was not Jewish. She did not follow Jewish law. She had heard of Jesus and believed with her whole heart He could heal her daughter. In a seemingly harsh manner, Jesus at first bluntly reminds her that she is not one of "the lost sheep of Israel" (v. 24) and is, therefore, not worthy of sharing in the family meal of God's grace. Her response exhibits great humility.

> *Even the dogs eat the crumbs that fall from their master's table.*
> *(Matthew 15:27)*

She knew that even the smallest portion of God's grace, through Jesus, was more than enough to satisfy her needs. She received her reward as Jesus revealed unlimited love and forgiveness for those with pure faith. Her daughter was healed.

Does it bother you that Jesus compares the woman to a dog? What would you have done? Would a look of irritation or offense come to your face? We live in a society that encourages us to elevate ourselves. Focusing on ourselves puts a barrier between us and Jesus. Approaching Him with a desire to put our problems on His table, we are rewarded with a sufficient serving. A spiritual scrap from the Master's table is a remarkable reward.

Dear Generous Savior,
To receive a mite of Your grace is
more than sufficient for me. Forgive
me when I elevate myself above
others and greedily expect more
than I deserve. I am grateful that
the scraps from Your table are a
coveted portion.
Amen.

A Hangry Field Trip

||||||||||||||||||||||||||||||||||||||||||||||

Matthew 14:1–17

Have you ever chaperoned an elementary school field trip? Maybe it was a day at the zoo with third graders or a hike through a nature center or arboretum with fifth graders? Fifty to one hundred, super-excited students escaped the confines of the school building and normal routines, ready for fresh air and outdoor instruction. Each one brought their own sack lunch to enjoy under the trees with their friends.

That's a happy scene. But what would happen if lunchtime came and the bus that held all the sack lunches was nowhere to be found? Hungry turns into whiny, whiny turns into cranky, and cranky turns into mayhem. The word *hangry* has become a popular way to describe how hunger fuels anger. No amount of classroom or field-trip volunteering would have prepared me to calm a crowd of hangry kids.

I have read and heard the story of Jesus feeding the five thousand many, many times. It is a common theme for Sunday school curriculum and sermon messages. At some point later in my life, the Spirit drew my attention to a not-so-small detail: The Bible says, "Five thousand men," but there were women and children there too (v. 21). That's not a crowd—that's a sporting event! A sporting event without the benefit of a sound system or a concession stand.

By the end of the day, the crowd was hungry. The disciples' solution? Send them home and let them take care of themselves (v. 15). Jesus's solution?

> *They do not need to go away. You give them something to eat.*
> *(Matthew 14:16)*

In a manner to which this classroom volunteer can relate, the disciples reacted with panic and doubt. Think of it . . . an impromptu picnic for more than five thousand people with five small loaves of bread and two small fish (v. 17). Isn't that a bit like saying, "Okay, third graders, I found one snack-size bag of fruit chews in my purse. Line up!"

What the disciples saw as a deficiency, Jesus saw as divine provision.

Have you ever been in a position to help someone but felt ill-equipped to solve the problem? Notice that in verse 16, Jesus doesn't say "feed them a four-course meal." He says "give them *something* to eat" (emphasis mine). God doesn't ask us to *solve* the problem. He asks us to *do something* to share His love with a person in need. No offering is too small when God blesses it.

Dear Father in heaven,
Thank You for providing for every one
of my needs. Thank You for sending
Jesus to show us how to accept what
You provide and to use Your gifts to
serve others. Give me Your Spirit of
compassion and mercy, and help me to
be generous with all I have.
Amen.

GLASS HALF-FULL

||||||||||||||||||||||||||||||||||||||||||

Luke 9:10–17

If you sat down at a table in a restaurant or someone's home and noticed the glass in front of you was half-filled, how would you react? Would you wonder if someone had already drunk from it? Perhaps the waitress or host was running low on a beverage and had to portion it among several people? Maybe your proclivity for spilling things was strategically preempted? Would you worry that you might become thirsty before you even finish your meal?

In the previous devotion, we focused on God's provision as Jesus fed the crowd of thousands. The second segment of the story, like the half-filled glass, separates the optimists from the pessimists.

When Jesus inquired about what means the disciples did have (glass half-full), they focused on the shortage (glass half-empty).

> *They answered, "We have only five loaves of bread and two fish—unless we go and buy food for all this crowd." (Luke 9:13)*

While this may be a pessimistic view, it's also a plausible statement. The disciples quickly worked themselves into a frenzy, even calculating how much it would cost them to buy food for the crowd (Mark 6:37).

I can relate. It doesn't take long for me to take my eyes off my omnipotent Father and start calculating everything that might go wrong. I can count even nonthreatening problems so quickly, the blessings in hand get ground to a pulp in my clenched fist.

It was only a few years ago that the description of what happened next really captured my attention.

> *Taking the five loaves and the two fish and looking up into heaven, he gave thanks and broke them. Then he gave them to the disciples to distribute to the people. (Luke 9:16)*

Jesus held in His hands the available food, acknowledged the Father by physically raising His eyes to heaven, humbly thanked the Father for it, divided it, and gave it away. Jesus didn't ask God to make enough for everyone. Jesus didn't question how this was possibly going to feed so many people. Jesus knew that God had provided what they needed in that moment and said grace.

Jesus chose to focus on the blessing that the Father had provided.

Instead of filling our heads and hearts and minds with pessimistic words like *small*, *only*, and *how*, God wants us to relax the clenched fist of our fears, allow Him to fill our hands with what we need, lift our eyes to Him, be grateful, share what we have, and optimistically watch Him multiply His grace.

Dear Heavenly Father,
Give me a spirit of contentment and
gratitude. Turn my negative, doubtful
thoughts into those of one who relies
wholly and confidently on You. Thank
You for providing my every need today.
Thank You for every blessing that goes
beyond my needs. Show me opportunities
to follow Your example and give to others.
Amen.

PICNIC BASKETS

||||||||||||||||||||||||||||||||||||||||||

Luke 9:17

I currently own three picnic baskets. The first is a beautiful wicker basket lined with blue-and-white gingham fabric that was a Mother's Day gift from my husband and son. The second is an antique metal picnic basket—really more of a lidded pail—in a blue, yellow, and orange plaid. The third is a large antique woven basket that I placed next to my reading chair to hold things like magazines, glasses, pencils, and sticky notes. This small collection could very easily become an obsession. I am especially attracted to the old baskets, as they seem to have stories to tell. Contemplating who might have used them and what food they transported makes for some imaginative and heart-warming tales.

In this final look at our Scripture readings about the feeding of the five thousand, a very unusual picnic is just wrapping up, and it is my favorite part of this account. The first devotion in this series taught us about God's provision of food. The second taught us to be grateful for what God has given us. This time we witness the abundance that accompanies God's grace.

> *They all ate and were satisfied, and the disciples picked up twelve basketfuls of broken pieces that were left over. (Luke 9:17)*

How many disciples? Twelve. How many basketfuls? Twelve. God provided food—enough to satisfy—plus leftovers.

My Condordia Self-Study Bible includes this study note:

> Bread was regarded by the Jews as a gift of God, and it was required that scraps that fell on the ground during a meal be picked up. The fragments were collected in small wicker baskets that were carried as a part of daily attire. (International Bible Society, 1984)

Wearable lunch boxes? Individual picnic baskets? Maybe all those Sunday school lessons were the true origin of my obsession with picnics!

The Gospel of Mark tells us this picnic took place near the Sea of Galilee (6:32), on green grass (6:39), they were satisfied (6:42), and there were leftovers (6:43). Basketfuls of leftovers. When was the last time you went to a picnic or potluck with an empty container and returned home with it full?

Often that is my experience with worship. I arrive empty or running on empty. God fills me with grace, love, and forgiveness through the Word and the sacraments. I leave restored. I am blessed and comforted and satisfied. What I lack, God provides. When God provides, He does so in abundance.

My basket is full. Is yours?

Dear Heavenly Father,
I raise my eyes to You and thank
You for the blessings You give. Jesus,
my Brother, teach me to see these
blessings as You do and to follow Your
example of faith and gratitude. Spirit,
my Friend, guide me to recognize the
potential of every blessing and waste
not one morsel of Your abundance.
Amen.

LEMONADE STANDS

IIIIIIIIIIIIIIIIIIIIIIIIIIIIIIIIIIIIIIIII

Luke 10:25–37

"Lemonade! Get your ice-cold lemonade!"

I have been known to drive around the block to buy a paper cup of lemonade from a couple entrepreneurs under the age of ten whenever and wherever those words reach my ears. Am I really that thirsty? No. Is the overly sweetened powdered beverage one of my greatest weaknesses? No. Do I know the proprietors? Probably not.

So why do I not only buy a cup but also generally double or quadruple their asking price?

One word: Gary.

Gary lived in our neighborhood when our boys were young. Whenever the boys dragged the card table and chairs outside, grabbed the poster board and markers, and started yelling down the street, Gary soon appeared. He would hang out with the boys for thirty minutes or more, talking about baseball and fishing. In that time, he would drink three or four cups of lemonade and eat at least that many scotcharoo bars (what can I say . . . we took this stuff seriously) and then hand the boys a ten-dollar bill. Jackpot!

To this day you cannot mention a lemonade stand to my boys without Gary's name entering the conversation. I'm sure the likelihood of a big tip was what made Gary's arrival at the stand so impressive then; but now, as they recall those memories, they remember his kindness.

> *But he wanted to justify himself, so he asked Jesus, "And who is my neighbor?" (Luke 10:29)*

In the parable of the good Samaritan, the Pharisees, the teachers of the law, wanted Jesus to narrow down—logistically, religiously, practically—who exactly qualified as their "neighbor." They wanted to put a limit on who they were to love so they could make sure to obey the letter of the law. Jesus gives examples of individuals who would be expected to help a stranger in need—a religious leader and a fellow countryman. Instead, these two passed by the opportunity, citing excuses. The third and most unexpected of heroes, a "foreigner" with more legitimate reasons to ignore the stranger, not only helps, but goes above and beyond the immediate need, extending kindness, time, effort, and compassion.

> *Love your neighbor as yourself. (Luke 10:27)*

Is buying a cup of lemonade comparable to saving someone's life? Certainly not. But let's not undermine the importance of showing kindness toward and taking an interest in the people God has placed around us. Taking those extra moments to ask those entrepreneurial kids what they are going to do with the money they make, if they made the lemonade themselves, or complimenting them on their manners will give them an example of how to be a good neighbor. An example they may never forget.

PS: I once bought a rock from some kids down the street when I thought they were selling lemonade. I would have preferred a scotcharoo, but I can't seem to resist pretty rocks either.

Dear Father,
Thank You for lemonade stands and the bright faces of children. Many times I do not know how to help people who truly need it. Please guide me to do what is right and go above and beyond in caring for others.
Amen.

THE LIFESAVING DELIVERY

||||||||||||||||||||||||||||||||||||||||

1 Samuel 17:17–18

As the youngest of three children in our farming family, I was often asked to deliver things. One of my earliest tasks involved taking kitchen scraps out to the barn to feed the barn cats. Running letters out to or retrieving the newspaper, bills, and letters from the mailbox wasn't too bad until it rained . . . or snowed. My brothers were always happy to see me, as long as I had food and drink in my hands. I became quite the asset when I learned the difference between a flat-head and a Phillips-head screwdriver! The small jobs often fall to the youngest.

Are you familiar with the Old Testament stories about David? Do you remember King David? Or war-hero David? There's also creative David, who played the harp and wrote poetry. Let's not disregard shepherd boy and giant slayer. How often, though, do you hear the story of David the delivery boy?

Before David ever hears the name Goliath, his father sends him on an errand. The youngest of eight brothers, David is sent to check on the safety of his brothers, who were engaged in battle with the Philistines. He didn't go empty handed.

> *Now Jesse said to his son David, "Take this ephah of roasted grain and these ten loaves of bread for your brothers and hurry to their camp. Take along these ten cheeses to the commander of their unit." (1 Samuel 17:17–18)*

An ephah is a measurement equivalent to a bushel, or about eight gallons. While we don't know anything else about the cheese, I'm guessing they weren't the little blocks of cheese we buy in the grocery store. Ten loaves of bread, ten blocks (or maybe wheels) of cheese, and a bushel of grain? That's a big picnic basket to carry for fifteen miles!

While delivering food, David heard Goliath's arrogant threats against the people of Israel and "the armies of the living God" (v. 26). He was disgusted that anyone would dare to speak against God. He stepped up. With a slingshot, a stone, and the name of God, David killed Goliath. No armor, helmet, shield, or sword. He stepped forward with faith and courage . . . and a picnic basket.

His task was to take sustenance to his brothers. God presented that delivery boy with an opportunity. David saw the chance to rescue others and glorify God.

And God delivered David.

Sometimes we may feel the small tasks placed before us lack importance. Our employment may not have us in the influential role we expected or desired. The help we give to others often can feel incomplete. Turn to God and say a prayer that the work you are doing, the donation you are giving, or even the pie you are making will create a giant opportunity for someone to see God at work.

Dear Living God,
You see my potential, and You give
me opportunities to deliver the
good news. Forgive me when I lack
confidence in You to guide my daily
steps. Help me to listen to Your
Spirit when He asks me to be brave
and faithful.
Amen.

Lunchroom Drama

|||||||||||||||||||||||||||||||||||||||||||

Luke 15:1–7

If ever there was a playground for teenage drama, it would have to be the school lunchroom. Some are large and modern, others are small and basic, but few are ever calm and quiet. Tables are islands inhabited by diners with common interests. A tacit map identifies the turf of social groups.

In the 1985 movie *The Breakfast Club*, five high school students spend one day together in detention. Each character represents a stereotypical teenage clique: a jock, a nerd, a punk, a snob, and a dweeb. At lunchtime each endures the scrutiny of the others based on the contents of their lunch. On an ordinary day, these five students would never consider sitting at the same lunch table; each would sit with their friends in their comfort zone. Forced to share a space and a meal, they break down the stereotypes and find they are more alike than ever imagined.

Even in biblical times, sharing a meal was a sign of friendship, of association. Being seen in the company of the wrong crowd was detrimental to your standing in society. The Pharisees, who considered themselves irreproachable in observing Jewish law, saw Jesus choosing to eat with the outcasts—corrupt tax collectors, adulterers, robbers, etc. It was an inconceivable act. (Spoiler alert: even more shocking than the snob and the punk in the movie becoming a couple.)

> *But the Pharisees and the teachers of the law muttered, "This man welcomes sinners and eats with them." (Luke 15:2)*

Some versions of the Bible use words like *mumbled, complained, grumbled,* and *whispered,* but I don't think any of those give the imagery the word *muttered* does. Can't you almost feel the negative, gossipy, belittling vibes radiating off those men as they huddle together in their group? Have you ever felt that vibe directed at you? Do you have to reach back into your memory bank for those lunchroom days? Or is there a more recent memory of being judged? Have you ever been called names for doing what is right and good or not going along with the crowd? We are frequently encouraged and even pressured to conform to the world's standards.

Jesus had different standards. He had no reservations about eating with the jocks, the nerds, the punks, the snobs, or the dweebs. His acceptance, His grace, His sacrifice was and is for every single sinner in equal portions. He knows the inadequacies, insecurities, deficiencies, and shortcomings of every one of us.

The movie ends with the reading of a required essay from the students. Their final statement is, "What we found out is that each one of us is a brain, and an athlete, and a basket case, a princess, and a criminal."[2] We are all sinners. Jesus loves and forgives us. He eats with us.

Dear Jesus,
You know me so well. You know my weaknesses, insecurities, fears, and my personal struggle with sin. Thank You for choosing to sit at my table as my friend and my Savior. Help me to learn from You to find the good in others and to eliminate my sinful mutterings about others.
Amen.

---

2   John Hughes, writer and director, *The Breakfast Club* (Los Angeles: Universal Pictures, 1985), film.

Muscle Memory

||||||||||||||||||||||||||||||||||||||
Luke 24:13–35

One of my favorite foodie movies is *Julie & Julia*. It is a fictional story based on the life of Julia Child. After moving to France with her husband, she enrolled in Le Cordon Bleu to cure her boredom and feel productive. In one of her first classes, she is seen woefully trying to chop an onion while her male classmates and instructor watch in disdain. That evening her husband finds her in the kitchen, ferociously and skillfully chopping onion after onion with the tear-inducing fumes preventing his entrance. She calmly walks into class the next day and out-chops the class with confidence.

Have you ever watched a cooking show and marveled at the knife skills of the chefs? A dull knife is the enemy of quick and consistent chopping. If you are like me though, a sharp knife is the enemy of my fingers! How do they make it look so easy?

Repetition.

Muscle memory is the term used to describe the commitment of an action to memory through repetition. When someone repeats a task so regularly, it becomes second nature. They don't even think about *how* to do it . . . their mind and hands automatically work together to create something amazing.

After Jesus's crucifixion, two disciples were walking down a road to a town called Emmaus. They were talking about Jesus, what He had taught them and the now empty grave. Jesus, having already revealed

His resurrected self to others, joins these two men on their journey. For whatever reason, they didn't recognize Him. He asks them questions about their conversation. They are baffled that this stranger has no concept of the mysterious current events in Jerusalem. He reveals the Scriptures to them, reminding them of all the messianic prophecies and signs that had been fulfilled. They *still* don't recognize Him.

As the day comes to a close, they invite this stranger to stay with them. They sit down to eat, and Jesus jostles their memory.

> *He took bread, gave thanks, broke it and began to give it to them. (Luke 24:30)*

In that moment they recognized Jesus. The next verse says their "eyes were opened." It is in the very act that Jesus has repeatedly performed in the company of His disciples that they recognize Him. Over and over again Jesus took bread, gave thanks, broke it, and gave it to His followers.

Muscle memory in action is an act of passion and devotion. Someone can explain every single detail of how to execute a task and it can make all the sense in the world, but it doesn't become personal until we see it in action. And then we must practice. Take hold of the life of Christ Jesus. Give thanks for His life and His brokenness. Share His story and His love with others. Share your story of God's faithfulness to you. The more you practice, the sooner it will become a recognizable part of you.

Dear Bread of Life,
Thank You for opening my eyes to
Your glory. Help me to recognize You
in the hands of others. Be with me as
I practice telling others about You.
Amen.

Omitting Ingredients

||||||||||||||||||||||||||||||||||||||||||

Exodus 12

anana cream pie: Oh, how I love it! So when before a weekend visit to my mom and dad, my mom asked if there was anything special I was hungry for, I quickly said, "Banana cream pie." We arrived, shared our hugs and greetings, and found the most beautiful pie sitting on the cupboard, crowned with peaks of lightly caramelized meringue.

As that first bite hit our tongues, we each paused. A look of contained shock crossed each face. Glances were exchanged. Not a single groan of appreciation was heard. Mom sat down and took her first bite. She looked around the table, as puzzled as everyone else. Then her eyes opened wide as the most unwelcome thought entered her mind. Her elbow hit the table, her head dropped into her hand, and she quietly said, "I forgot the sugar."

Very quickly our confusion turned to sympathetic reassurances and then to mutual laughter. How that pie turned out so beautifully without a speck of sugar remains a mystery. Had it turned out perfectly sweetened as expected, we surely would have enjoyed every bite and been grateful. It is unlikely, though, that we would still be talking about that pie today. The absence of one ingredient created a treasured memory.

Throughout the Bible, God's people celebrate with great reverence the Passover instituted in Exodus 12. A symbolic menu was prepared and repeated each year in remembrance of their delivery from slavery in Egypt. There was to be roasted lamb, bitter herbs, and unleavened bread.

> *Celebrate the Festival of Unleavened Bread, because it was on this very day that I brought your divisions out of Egypt. Celebrate this day as a lasting ordinance for the generations to come. In the first month you are to eat bread made without yeast, from the evening of the fourteenth day until the evening of the twenty-first day. (Exodus 12:17–18)*

Bread made without yeast is unleavened. It is the bread of haste. The Israelites had to be ready at a moment's notice to leave the land of captivity. Sharing this same meal taught generation after generation the story of God's power, grace, and love. It was a consumable story of sacrifice and protection, a treasured memory for generations of God's people.

As Christians, we celebrate Holy Communion. Each time we receive the bread and wine, the body and blood of our Savior, we too remember. We remember we are forgiven, protected, and loved.

We can share our own stories of God's forgiveness and faithfulness with others. I'm quite certain my mom never expected that one disappointing pie failure would, decades later, inspire a devotion. I think it was an unintentional, but inspired, omission. I just wish I could also share a piece of her fully sweetened banana cream pie with you!

Dear Bread of Heaven,
Thank You for not only providing
deliverance for the Israelites but also
a meal to commemorate Your love
for Your people. May I always see
Holy Communion as an opportunity
to remember, to witness, and to share.
When I eat the unleavened bread,
remind me there is no time to waste.
Come soon, Lord.
Amen.

Pancake Sundays

||||||||||||||||||||||||||||||||||||||||
Matthew 25:35

I t isn't very often a commercial has an uplifting, meaningful message. When one with character and kindness appears, my sentimental nature gets a boost. A few years ago, a home furnishings store shared a message with all these attributes.

A family moves into an apartment building. To get to know their new neighbors, they distribute posters made by the young daughter inviting everyone to Pancake Sundays. The sign, decorated in crayon with rainbows, hearts, and flowers, simply says:

Pancake Sundays
Free Pancakes
Apt 5D

The next Sunday they hear a soft knock. Opening the door, the family sees a young couple hesitantly holding up the invitation. The couple is welcomed inside, and they all eat together at a table. Each week more people knock on the door, and the table is extended. The dishes are mismatched in that irritating way that looks really good. Pancakes, bacon, sausage, and fruit are passed around from neighbor to neighbor. Eventually everyone is participating, except the neighbor in 5C—an older man with a grumpy, leave-me-alone vibe.

The empty place at the table troubles the girl, so she fills a plate, takes it to his door, places it in front of his apartment, knocks, and leaves. The man opens his door to see this act of kindness, and his grumpiness dissolves. He picks up his plate, takes it to apartment 5D, and knocks. The look on the girl's face when she hears the knock is pure joy. The table will be full.

> *For I was hungry and you gave me something to eat, I was thirsty and you gave me something to drink, I was a stranger and you invited me in, I needed clothes and you clothed me, I was sick and you looked after me, I was in prison and you came to visit me. (Matthew 25:35–36)*

This passage is part of a parable Jesus is telling to explain to the disciples how to live their faith. A parable is often described as an earthly story with a heavenly or spiritual lesson. It describes the lifestyle of a Christian: generous, hospitable, compassionate, caring, empathetic, attentive, and kind. It is easy for me to think that I would most certainly do anything for Jesus. But would I do any of these things for a neighbor? Or for a stranger?

The parable continues with the explanation that acts of true compassion are completed with no thought of personal gain. They are done purely out of love. A love that comes from knowing the Father, the Son, and the Holy Spirit. When that love lives within us, our only motivation for serving others is the hope that Christ's light will shine through us. Our actions can bring joy, peace, and faith to our neighbors, far and wide.

Sincere intentions, simple kindnesses—sometimes in the form of pancakes or a handwritten invitation. Whose "door" could you "knock" on today?

Holy Spirit,
Open my eyes today to see the needs
of those around me. When You knock
on the door of my soul, help me to
accept Your invitation to practice
compassion, kindness, and comfort.
Amen.

Quarts, Pints, and Jelly Jars

||||||||||||||||||||||||||||||||||||||||

2 Kings 4:1-7

Canning jars have become a novelty. People use them to decorate their house, as flower vases, and to prepare single-serve salads for easy-to-grab lunches. When I was a kid, these ideas would have made me shake my head in disbelief.

For us, canning jars had one role: to be filled and sealed with fruits, vegetables, and meats. The sight of row after row of empty glass jars in my parents' cold room—the farmhouse equivalent of a wine cellar, but for food—indicated two things:

- It must be spring, as we've spent the winter enjoying wonderful meals made from the contents of those jars.
- Very soon we will be spending hour after hour harvesting produce from our large garden and filling and sealing every jar we can find.

The reward for all our work was seeing those cold-room shelves loaded with jars full of potential, a rainbow of possibilities. We certainly weren't going to starve!

I say this with a bit of sarcasm. My parents grew up in an era where farm families did worry about having enough to eat from year to year. Canning was a necessity. Preserving whatever was available and not wasting a thing was a way of life.

This concern is amplified to desperation in 2 Kings. A widow, whose husband was a student of the Word of God, was about to lose everything: land to unscrupulous creditors, sons to slavery, and her own security to cultural mores. She reached out to Elisha, the prophet who served as her husband's professor. His guidance came in the form of a question.

> *How can I help you? Tell me, what do you have in your house? (2 Kings 4:2)*

Her response is so typical of us all: nothing, except . . .

"I don't have anything! Well, technically, I do have [fill in the blank]. But what good will that do?"

Where we see a limit, God sees potential. This widow only had a little olive oil. Elisha gave her and her sons simple instructions:

- collect empty jars from your neighbors (ask for help),
- get as many as you can (trust),
- go inside and shut the door (let God show you His power),
- and start pouring the oil you have into the jars (believe).

The widow's oil flowed until the last jar was filled, providing enough oil to pay their debts and extra to sell for their own needs.

What have you seen recently as an empty jar in your life? Was it a relationship, a talent, a means of security, an emotion? Does it feel like there is no solution? Have you asked God to take what you do have and fill those jars of potential?

Focus on what you do have. Imagine taking hold of that and using it in the most trusting and faithful way by pouring it into that first jar of potential. Don't worry about the second or the third or the twentieth jar. Fill the first jar and watch how the "oil" flows.

Just don't forget to sterilize your "jars" with trust and faith!

Dear God,
You gave me special gifts. Forgive me when
I undermine their value. I want to be filled
with Your wisdom and prepared to share
the story of Your impact on my life.
Amen.

Regretfully Decline or Joyfully Accept?

||||||||||||||||||||||||||||||||||||||||||||

Luke 14:15-23

Do you like parties? I am a *big* fan. There's excitement in seeing a pretty envelope in the mailbox among the bills and junk mail. A celebration is in the works. Birthday parties, graduations, weddings, baby showers . . . happy occasions with friends and food! Save me the corner piece of cake! You know, the one with all the bonus frosting.

Oftentimes an invitation will come with a request to RSVP— a French phrase, *Répondez s'il vous plaît*, meaning "please respond." The hosts want to plan for the right amount of space, food, and accommodations. They know not everyone they invite will be able to attend. Conflicts are inevitable. Distance and travel expenses may be prohibitive.

Sometimes, however, the reasons are more like excuses.

- I have so many graduation parties that day!
- I have no idea why they would invite me . . . we're not close.
- That was the only free weekend on the calendar all summer!
- They won't even notice if I'm not there.

There are lots of understandable reasons and debatable excuses to check the "will not attend" box. It's only after the celebration that regret might set in.

What if, a few days after the party, everyone around you was talking about it being the best time they've had in years. Or imagine hearing later that your absence was not only noticed but also a true disappointment. Perhaps your presence held great meaning for the host, of which you simply weren't aware. How would you feel to learn the reception was so poorly attended that the host was left with disappointment instead of fond memories? Suddenly that "will not attend" response feels like a big mistake.

Jesus tells a parable about a king who prepares a wedding banquet. The invitations go out, and the excuses are abundant.

> *But they all alike began to make excuses. The first said, "I have just bought a field, and I must go and see it. Please excuse me." Another said, "I have just bought five yoke of oxen, and I'm on my way to try them out. Please excuse me." Still another said, "I just got married so I can't come." (Luke 14:18–20)*

Those who should have felt honored to receive the invitation declined. The king expands the guest list, but the response is just as apathetic. Finally the king extends invitations to strangers: the poor, the lame, the outcast. The banquet hall was filled. Those who chose to attend were given the gift of the king's favor.

God invites everyone to accept His Son through faith. The "banquet" of eternal life is waiting for each of us. Some will "Joyfully Accept" and others will "Regretfully Decline." You *are* invited. He is saving you a place! Make no mistake. He loves you so much that your absence from this feast will be a great disappointment to the Host.

Have you sent Him your RSVP yet?

Dear Father in heaven,
I am blessed to be invited to Your
heavenly banquet. When I speak
of Your faithfulness, may my words
always be so sincere that those who
hear them will also joyfully accept
Your invitation.
Amen.

Set an Extra Place at the Table

||||||||||||||||||||||||||||||||||||

1 Kings 17:1–16

Growing up on a farm, one of my earliest responsibilities was setting the table. It is important to note this was not a task required only for Sunday dinners or random weeknight meals. Mom prepared breakfast, dinner, and supper for us—each one a sit-down gathering. My job was to place five plates, five sets of silverware, five glasses, napkins, salt and pepper, and butter on the table before my dad and brothers came in from working outside.

Once in a while my mom would say, "Set an extra place at the table." This was the sign that we had extra help on the farm, or my grandmother had come out to work with my mom and me in the garden, or someone had stopped by to return something borrowed from my dad. The phrase "stay for supper" flowed from my parents' lips without hesitation. They never worried about not having enough to eat. It was common courtesy to serve the guest first.

It might not be difficult to imagine portioning out a meal to include one extra person unless that meal is already meager. Growling stomachs are seldom concerned with hospitality and good manners when the food supply is stretched thin. This was the dilemma that faced a woman and the Old Testament prophet Elijah.

Elijah was a traveling bad-news bearer. God sent him far and wide warning people about troubles ahead. God was his travel agent, and Elijah's journey was no five-star cruise. His food and water came from sources like ravens, streams, and strangers. Elijah, instructed by God, asks a poor, dying widow for food.

Even after she admits to having only enough for one small meal for her and her son, Elijah says those faith-building words:

> *Don't be afraid. Go home and do as you have said. But first make a small loaf of bread for me from what you have and bring it to me, and then make something for yourself and your son. (1 Kings 17:13)*

Notice how Elijah instructs her to feed him first. Good manners aside, in the widow's place, I think I would have given him the stink eye. And maybe she did. But with Elijah's assurance that the flour and oil would sustain her and her son until the end of the drought, she followed his instructions. Welcome to the kitchen where the jars of flour and oil were bottomless. That drought lasted over three years. She prepared one cake for a stranger, and the results of her generosity lasted for years.

Opportunities to serve others are all around us. We need not worry whether what we have to share will be enough. When we trust God completely, He will provide. He has already prepared a way for our acts of generosity to become miracles.

Just set an extra place at the table.

Dear Faithful Father,
May the sight and taste of bread and
oil always be a reminder to me that
Your mercy is bottomless. Thank You
for sending Jesus, the Bread of Life,
to save me from my doubts, fears, and
sin. Go ahead of me and lead me to
serve others first.
Amen.

Stars and Candy Bars

||||||||||||||||||||||||||||||||||||||||||||||||

Luke 15:11–32

Long, long ago, in a gymnasium not far away, an event occurred that to this day makes me a bit ashamed. The only thing keeping this event from shaming me completely is the fact that the fit I threw somehow managed to stay in my head instead of taking its usual route . . . bypassing my brain completely and exiting my mouth.

You need to know one thing about me to fully understand this situation. I am a nonathlete. Being a "late bloomer" (anybody else scarred by that term?) and uncoordinated, as much as I wanted to be an athlete, it just wasn't in the cards. I tried hard: basketball, softball, track, golf, bowling, tag . . . don't *even* ask me about Red Rover. Virtually everyone who shared my last name excelled at some sport. I tried to make up for my weaknesses by never giving the coaches a reason to doubt my devotion. I was never, ever absent or tardy.

At the end of one basketball season, we had a team awards party. The award for perfect attendance was a construction-paper star with your name on it. The award for receiving the most fouls? A giant candy bar.

Are you kidding me? You do something wrong over and over again, and you get the best reward? My inability to fully grasp the concept of rewarding hustle and aggressiveness was yet another sign I had no business on the court.

I hated that construction-paper star. I was jealous. The paper star felt cheap and disposable, like an afterthought. If the candy bar had been standard sized instead of the giant, enviable chunk of chocolate, I wouldn't have reacted so poorly. Most likely it was the attention given to the award winner that I envied. Regardless, I felt slighted.

Jesus tells a parable about a father who has two sons. The younger son boldly asks for his share of the estate. He leaves home, commits a bunch of fouls, and squanders all he has received. Embarrassed and repentant, he returns home, and his father throws a party.

The older, responsible, dutiful (and I'm guessing, very prompt) son is furious.

> *But he answered his father, "Look! All these years I've been slaving for you and never disobeyed your orders. Yet you never gave me even a young goat so I could celebrate with my friends." (Luke 15:29)*

Can't you just hear him? "A *feast*! You're going to prepare a *feast* for *him* after all the stupid, sinful, wasteful things he has done? Why would you reward him for that?" Much like the older brother, I threw a pity party because I felt I deserved more. What a selfish attitude.

Self-centered is another way to describe sin. We compare ourselves to others. Sometimes we "win" and sometimes we "lose." The fact is, God doesn't compare you to me or me to you. He loves each of us completely and unconditionally. He created us to be unique. He wants only for us to turn to Him and, if necessary, *re*-turn to Him. He wants to celebrate, to prepare a feast for us at His eternal table.

No doubt that feast will be unimaginably more satisfying than any candy bar.

Dear God,
You see me at my best and my
worst. I am both the dutiful and the
disobedient child. I do not deserve Your
compassion or a seat at Your eternal
table. Even so, You have my place
prepared, and I thank You. Help me to
see every person as You see them, and
help them find their way to You.
Amen.

STONE SOUP

||||||||||||||||||||||||||||||||||||||||
Genesis 25:27–34

*S*tone Soup, an old European folk story and children's book, tells the tale of hungry travelers who entice strangers with the crazy concept of soup made with water and rocks. Curiosity convinces each stranger to contribute to the pot, improving the flavor of the soup. Small offerings of carrots, herbs, potatoes, onions, and meat are added, and the stone is removed. The characters share a nurturing meal with each other and a positive lesson with readers of all ages.

Can you imagine being so hungry you would gladly accept a bowl of "stone" soup? Can you imagine being so hungry that, in a moment of weakness, you would give up your entire inheritance? In the very first book of the Bible, a man named Esau did just that.

> *Once when Jacob was cooking some stew, Esau came in from the open country, famished. He said to Jacob, "Quick, let me have some of that red stew! I'm famished!" (Genesis 25:29–30)*

As the oldest son of Isaac and Rebekah, Esau was entitled to the birthright. A skillful hunter arriving home from his work, he was *famished*. His twin but slightly younger brother, Jacob, prepared the meals. Sounds like a convenient arrangement, doesn't it? Having such complementary talents and interests, these guys should have appreciated and respected each other.

Unfortunately, dissension between these boys began before they were even born. During Rebekah's pregnancy, she felt the babies wrestling within her. As parents, Isaac and Rebekah were divided by the favoritism they displayed: Isaac loved Esau, but Rebekah loved Jacob. Jacob used Esau's hunger to exchange a bowl of stew for the birthright. Not only was Esau relinquishing his inheritance, but he was also rejecting the covenant promises of his ancestors for a meal.

The animosity, feuding, and deception between these parents and children continued. On his deathbed, Isaac unknowingly bestows his blessing on Jacob instead of Esau. Isaac's last meal was served with a side of trickery and deceit, fueling Esau's hatred and causing Jacob to flee his land.

Two stories, one childhood fiction and one biblical truth, about soup. The first teaches the benefits of working together, and the second teaches the destruction of division. However, both stories involve deception. All the characters are sinful human beings, just like us. Even in our hunger for worldly fairness and respect, God satisfies us. We know His will far exceeds our understanding. God removes the stone of sin from our lives and encourages us to share, cooperate, and commune with all our sinful but fiercely loved brothers and sisters in Christ.

Dear God,
There are many times when I cannot
understand why things happen the
way they do. I get frustrated when
situations are not fair or justice is not
served. Remind me that Your ways
are not the world's ways and Your
purposes supersede my desires for my
own good. Help me to always have a
generous and helpful spirit.
Amen.

Superpowers

||||||||||||||||||||||||||||||||||||||

John 2:1–11

Have you ever been asked which superpower you would most like to have? Typical answers often include being in two places at the same time, time travel, flight, etc. In one episode of a popular television sitcom, this question was posed, and the character's answer gave me a big laugh. She said, "Not to steal from the Bible, but turning water into wine sounds pretty good."[2]

It does, doesn't it? Grab a glass, put it under the faucet, fill it with water, and presto-change-o . . . wine! And not just wine but the *best* wine. No more worrying over the perfect wine to pair with a meal or if you will have enough for your next party.

Modern-day technology and convenience have blurred our ability to fully comprehend the amazing superpower Jesus exercised at a wedding in Cana. Picture the setting of Jesus's first miracle: a wedding lasting for seven days, guests who have likely traveled on foot to stay with you, no refrigeration, no running water.

No running water.

Verse 6 tells us there were six stone jars nearby, each holding twenty to thirty gallons. As required by Jewish law, they held water to

2 *Big Bang Theory*, season 8, episode 16, "The Intimacy Acceleration," directed by Mark Cendrowski, created by Chuck Lorre and Bill Prady, aired February 26, 2015, on CBS, https://www.imdb.com/title/tt3862714/.

be used for ceremonial washing. Large amounts of water would have to be retrieved from the nearest source, well in advance, to accommodate such a crowd.

Mary approaches her son for help when she discovers the host family has run out of wine. This is not a here-are-the-keys-to-my-car-run-to-the-store-and-buy-a-few-cases-of-wine-to-help-them-through-the-end-of-the-night kind of request. Think of the time commitment wine-*making* requires: the vines, the grapes, the harvest, the fermenting, the aging. Maybe this is why Jesus asks Mary why she is involving Him. What did she think He could do?

Clearly she believes He can do something.

> *His mother said to the servants, "Do whatever he tells you."* (John 2:5)

Don't ask questions, just follow His lead. Imagine their sarcastic glances when Jesus tells them to fill those large, heavy stone jars with water. They do it. They take some to the master of the banquet. The master proclaims this wine better than anything served so far. He doesn't know anything unusual has transpired. The bridal party doesn't know. The guests don't know. But the miracle is revealed to the servants. The servants and the disciples and Mary are the ones who witness Jesus's power. The party goes on, but the lives of those bystanders would never be the same.

What "jars" do you need to fill today? What tasks or errands seem so mundane? Would you be able to approach those tasks with a willing spirit if you knew that Jesus's superpowers might be working through you in that very moment? We don't always get to see the results of our service, but with Jesus they are truly transformed.

Dear Miracle Worker,
With a grateful heart, I will go about my
work today. May the work of my hands
benefit others and show Your love to them.
Fill me with Your Spirit and transform me.
Amen.

THE DISHWASHING FEUD

||||||||||||||||||||||||||||||||||||||||||||

Matthew 23:13-26

This is the story of a feud between my maternal grandmother and my husband's maternal grandmother. The two women never met. In fact, my grandmother passed away before I even met my husband. This "feud" exists only in my head and involves dirty dishes.

In elementary and junior high school, I spent many Saturdays at my grandmother's house. I would help her garden, clean, bake, quilt—whatever was on the list for that day. Washing dishes was always on the list. This woman knew that hot water killed germs; therefore, the rinse water was scalding hot. Seriously, she boiled water on the stove to periodically add to the rinse water. No germs were going to survive that bath. If my cousin and I happened to be at Grandma's house on the same day, we would argue over who "got" to wash and who "had" to rinse and dry.

Fast-forward ten or fifteen years to the first time I washed dishes with my husband's grandmother. It was my first holiday meal with his family. The table had been cleared, and I took my dishwashing skills to the kitchen to help. I managed to get the washing responsibilities (no one else seemed to care), and about ten plates into the process, my grandmother-in-law leaned over my shoulder and said, "You don't have to get *every* speck off the dishes. What do you think the *towel* is for?" I begged my grandmother's forgiveness and washed a little faster.

If the simple chore of cleaning dishes could confuse me so much, imagine the confusion of the teachers of the law when Jesus used it to condemn their hypocrisy.

> *Woe to you, teachers of the law and Pharisees, you hypocrites! You clean the outside of the cup and dish, but inside they are full of greed and self-indulgence. Blind Pharisee! First clean the inside of the cup and dish, and then the outside also will be clean. (Matthew 23:25–26)*

They were so concerned over keeping the letter of the law that they became filled with pride, judgment, arrogance, greed, and self-centeredness. They were clean on the outside but filthy and corrupt on the inside.

No matter if you wash your dishes in a sink of *really* hot water or load up an automatic dishwasher, we've all found the dish with a sparkling exterior that was exposed to all the water and soap and scrubbing but an inner crevice of baked-on cheese that did not get the attention it required. That spot is the hardest to clean and causes us the most frustration and effort. We each have those "crevices" inside that require some extra cleansing. God will show them to you, and He will give you the tools to eliminate all the "specks."

Sometimes it might take a little time in hot water or require a little extra polishing.

Dear Father,
Clean my heart, my mind, and my
spirit. Thank You for sending Jesus
to endure the heat and pressure of
death so His resurrection can free
me from the stains of sin. May I love
others so much that greed, hypocrisy,
arrogance, and judgment cannot
survive in my heart.
Amen.

The Essential Pantry

||||||||||||||||||||||||||||||||||||||||

Genesis 6:9–22

After more than twenty-five years of marriage, my husband and I moved from our starter home into a more modern and expansive space. Many aspects of this new place appealed to us, but one room in particular had my chef's heart pumping. Although the kitchen was beautiful and I couldn't wait to start cooking and baking in it, I was in love with the pantry.

Before Pinterest-worthy images start dancing through your head, this is a simple space. It was equipped with simple wire shelving, a few hooks for my aprons, and an electrical outlet. What was so exciting about a pantry? I think it was (and is) the opportunity to always have what I need on hand.

No matter how hard I try though, it never fails to amaze me when the one thing I need for a recipe or meal is absent from my pantry. There are three cans of evaporated milk on the shelf when a dessert requires sweetened condensed. The lasagna that is going to a sick neighbor relied on the box of lasagna noodles that is only half-full. Clearly I'd have to improve my meal-planning skills to have every single thing I need in that pantry for a whole month.

> *You are to take every kind of food that is to be eaten and store it away as food for you and for them. (Genesis 6:21)*

God put Noah in charge of building a massive boat in the presence of a mocking community to prepare for an unprecedented catastrophe. That boat had to be big enough for Noah's family of eight (at a minimum) and two of every species of land, sea, and air creature. Verse 19 ends with the words "to keep them alive with you."

He had to prepare for forty days and forty nights of rain while sequestered in a boat. That was how long it *rained*. A footnote in my Bible translates the timetables and reveals a total length of more than a year before Noah set foot on dry land (Genesis 8:14).

Noah needed a *big* pantry.

Take one minute to consider what it would take to feed just one animal for a year. Let's choose an adult pig as our example. It's not the biggest animal or the smallest. It doesn't have a complicated diet. An average pig will eat five pounds of meal or grain in a day. That is the equivalent of 1,825 pounds of food. Rounding up a little, that's one ton for one animal. Think about the meal-planning God required of Noah and his family.

While I have no doubt God's hand was active in every detail of the preparations and execution of His plan, verse 22 says "Noah did everything just as God commanded him." Noah gathered the guests, prepared the house, and filled the pantry.

Dear God of our Fathers,
Thank You for Noah and his example
of unwavering faithfulness. Fill me
with all that I need to carry out
Your plan for my life, and save me
from the floods of earthly desires that
threaten my devotion to You.
Amen.

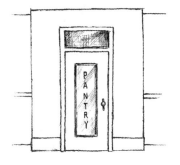

WISE MENU CHOICES

IIIIIIIIIIIIIIIIIIIIIIIIIIIIIIIIIIIIIIIIIII
Daniel 1:1–17

One summer ritual of my childhood was walking beans. If you are unfamiliar with this farming practice, consider yourself fortunate. Back in the day, soybean farmers and their "lucky" children removed invasive weeds from fields by walking up and down the rows, pulling or hoeing out the offenders. The job itself was tolerable until heat, humidity, mud, dirt, bugs, and annoying brothers contributed to your discomfort.

After working for a few hours, we found the shade of some trees or our truck and took a break. We looked forward to whatever my mom had brought for our snack or lunch. There was always water. Simple foods like fruit, quick breads, or small sandwiches were included. The last thing my parents needed were three grumpy (i.e., grumpier) kids moaning and groaning about stomachaches for the next several hours. Mom chose foods that would give us energy but not make us lethargic. If we kids had been left to pack our own snacks, I sincerely doubt we would have chosen so wisely.

When Jerusalem was besieged by the king of Babylon, Daniel and several other men were handpicked to serve him. They were to be treated well, even receiving food and wine from the king's table. But this food was not the food of their faith. They were to be served meals meant to tempt them and weaken their devotion to God. Food from the king's table had already been dedicated to the Babylonian gods.

Eating it signaled acceptance of those gods. These Israelite men had to decide what they were going to eat. Facing death for challenging the king's order, they chose to remain loyal to God. They requested a simple menu of vegetables and water, but the official in charge feared they would become too weak to perform their duties. Daniel proposed a ten-day diet challenge.

> *Please test your servants for ten days: Give us nothing but vegetables to eat and water to drink. Then compare our appearance with that of the young men who eat the royal food, and treat your servants in accordance with what you see. (Daniel 1:12–13)*

Their devotion and courage were rewarded by God, physically and mentally, and it did not go unnoticed. Healthier, bigger, and wiser, they were ready and able to assist the king. In fact, they were found to be ten times better than all the other advisors in the kingdom (v. 20).

Have you thought about the spiritual and physical nourishment you will need to handle the difficulties you may face today? Do you trust that God will see you through the peril you face when you acknowledge and follow His ways? Are you willing to give up some royal treatment to stay true to God's plan? Maybe it is time for each of us to look over today's menu and make wise choices.

Dear God,
Help me to make the best choices each
day so I can face the lions and fires
in my life without fear. Please give
me courage and strength to remain
loyal to You. Thank You for the Bible
stories that taught me when I was
young and continue to teach me now.
Amen.

GRATITUDE

||||||||||||||||||||||||||||||||||||||||

Oh give thanks unto the Lord
For He is good and His mercy endures forever!
Amen.

As a disciple of Christ, I am called to share the gospel. It's not easy. I guess I always pictured evangelism as walking right up to someone and asking them if they believe in God. Thinking about that now, I understand my own immaturity in this assumption. There are many ways to share faith. Chatty by nature, I never imagined I would share my faith in written form! I am so grateful God presented this opportunity to me.

By telling these stories, my hope is that I have created a memoir of my faith for my family, friends, and anyone who picks up this book to read even a single page. Should my husband and I be blessed with grandchildren and great-grandchildren, may this book provide them with an opportunity to hear some light-hearted stories of their ancestors and the deep-felt connection they had with the almighty God.

My gratitude extends also to some amazing people who helped me find my way to and through this book.

- My mom: the most selfless, humble, and faithful person I know. Thank you for starting each day of my childhood with devotions, ending each day with prayers, placing an Advent wreath at the center of our Christmas decorations, teaching me how to cook and bake with love, and for always, always reminding me to Whom I belong.

- Marty: my husband. You crack me up, rein me in, lead "from the back," and never let me down. Thank you for standing with me in the hardest of times, sharing joy in the little things, and loving the imperfect me. It is because you encouraged me to take a different path that this book exists.
- Nick: my son, my social media guru, and the reason I officially started writing. Thank you for taking me over the hurdle of creating a blog and for answering my parade of questions with patience and humor. Your creativity and drive motivate me, and your ability to find the best of every situation is a true gift.
- Marcus: my son, my artist, and the one who has taught me all about perspective. Thank you for inspiring me to look more closely at nature, art, and movies and discover the beauty in the details. I am so grateful that you agreed to illustrate this book and share your talent here. The messages of this book are more inviting and intriguing because of your work.
- Pastor Marti Nalean: my friend, my accountability partner, and my spiritual editor. I am so grateful for your guidance and advice throughout the writing of this book. You encouraged me with kindness, clarified my cluttered thoughts, and corrected my words when they failed to convey the true message.
- Judy Hagey: It is a brave woman who willingly accepts the challenge of editing a manuscript from a writer whose educational background involved as few language arts classes as possible. Thank you for caring about grammar, punctuation, and sentence structure, and all those things that I should have cared more about in college. I am grateful for your talents, wisdom, and guidance.

Thank you for choosing this book. I pray you learned something new and are inspired to spend more time discovering how God will speak to you through the Bible and through the gentle nudges of the Holy Spirit. May God inspire you to share with others what He has done in your life . . . because that is a story only you can tell.

ORDER INFORMATION

To order additional copies of this book, please visit:
www.redemption-press.com
picniclifefoodie.com
Also available on Amazon.com and BarnesandNoble.com
or by calling toll-free 1-844-2REDEEM.

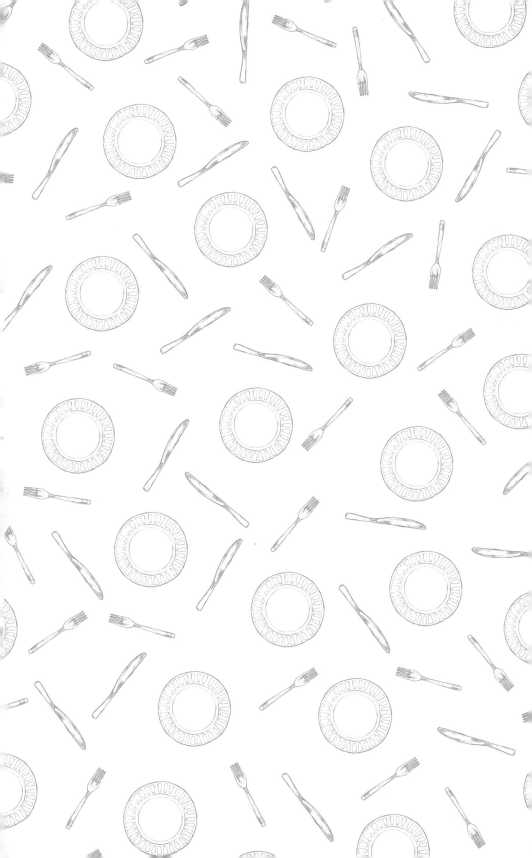

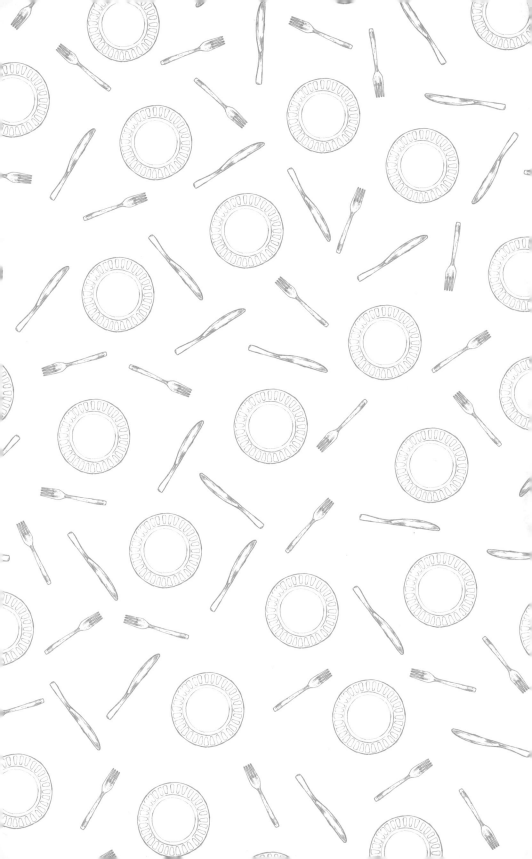